◁ **Overleaf** A view over the old city of Jerusalem in Israel. The city is sacred to Jews, Christians and Muslims alike.

◀ **These beautiful patterns of tiles** are from the Dome of the Rock in Jerusalem. The Dome is a sacred shrine for Muslims, who believe that it is from here that the Prophet Muhammad ascended into heaven.

YOUR WORLD EXPLAINED

Religions

An accessible guide that *really*
explains the world's faiths

ANITA GANERI

MARSHALL PUBLISHING • LONDON

A Marshall Edition
Conceived, edited and designed by
Marshall Editions Ltd
The Orangery
161 New Bond Street
London W1Y 9PA

First published in the UK in 1997 by Marshall Publishing Ltd
This edition published in 1998

ISBN 1-84028-155-3

Editor: Steve Setford
Designers: Frances de Rees, Siân Williams
Design Manager: Ralph Pitchford
Managing Editor: Kate Phelps
Art Director: Branka Surla
Editorial Director: Cynthia O'Brien
Production: Janice Storr, Selby Sinton
Picture Research: Elizabeth Loving
Research: Michaela Moher

Originated in Singapore by Master Image
Printed and bound in Portugal by Printer Portuguesa

Contents

ANCIENT RELIGIONS

PEOPLE OF THE BOOK

INTRODUCTION

THIS BOOK IS AN INTRODUCTION TO THE WORLD'S RELIGIONS, both the ancient beliefs of the past and the living faiths of today. Some religions are worldwide faiths with millions of followers, while others are the local beliefs of a particular area or group of people.

What is religion?

In ancient times, people tried to explain the world around them as the work of the gods. This is how religion began, with prayers and thanks being offered to the gods of nature for the gifts of the sun, rain and crops that enabled people to survive. Today, there are many different religions, with a wide variety of beliefs and ways of worship. Most religions, however, share the common purpose of trying to explain the mysteries of life: how the world was created, why it was created, what happens to people when they die and why there is suffering in the world.

▲ **In the Hindu religion,** bathing in the sacred water of the River Ganges is believed to wash away a person's sins. Worshippers offer prayers to the gods as they bathe

Beliefs and worship

At the centre of many religions is the worship of a god or gods. These are holy, spiritual beings who are believed to have power over people's lives and actions. Many people speak to their gods through prayer, either at home or in a place of worship such as a church, mosque or temple. In some religions, priests conduct services and ceremonies, speaking to the gods on behalf of the worshippers and acting as spiritual guides. Most religions provide their followers with a code for life – that is, a set of rules to help them lead a better life on Earth and in any afterlife that might exist.

◄ **This Jewish boy** is reading from the scriptures. Many faiths have their own scriptures, which are special books or texts that contain teachings and stories, and set out the rules by which their followers should live their lives.

Working together

Over the centuries, the differences between the major religions have caused many conflicts. Most religions

8

now try to live and work more peacefully together. They emphasise the beliefs they have in common, rather than the differences between them, and teach their followers tolerance and respect for people of other faiths and beliefs.

Dates

In this book, the abbreviations B.C.E. ("Before the Common Era") and C.E. ("Common Era") are used before and after dates. They are used instead of the abbreviations B.C. ("Before Christ") and A.D., (*Anno Domini*, meaning "In the Year of our Lord"), which are based on the Christian calendar.

▶ **This carving** decorates the front of the Cathedral of St. James in Santiago de Compostela, Spain. Thousands of Christians flock to the city each year to visit St. James' shrine.

A GUIDE TO THE RELIGIOUS SYMBOLS USED IN THIS BOOK

Throughout this book, different symbols are used to represent the different religions. Some of these symbols have a special meaning for the religion and its followers. These are explained below. They are often used on flags, banners and cards. Other symbols are used to make the religion easier to recognise and remember.

The six-pointed Star of David is the best-known symbol of Judaism. It appears on the flag of the Jewish state of Israel.

The symbol of Christianity is the cross. It reminds Christians that Jesus Christ died on a cross to save the world from sin.

The star and crescent moon are the symbols of Islam. They often appear on the flags of Muslim countries. Green is the Islamic colour.

This Hindu symbol represents the sacred sound Om. It is believed to contain the secrets of the universe and is often chanted in prayers.

The symbol of Jainism is a wheel within a hand. The wheel represents the cycle of birth and rebirth, of which every person is a part.

Zoroastrian worship centres around the sacred fire, which represents righteousness and truth. It is always kept burning in temples and homes.

The eight spokes of the Buddhist Wheel of Life represent the points of the Noble Eight-fold Path, a vital part of the Buddha's teaching.

The Sikh symbol is called the Ek-Onkar. It is used to represent the one God in whom the Sikhs believe.

This is the Chinese character for China, which is sometimes used to represent the ancient Chinese religion of Confucianism.

The Taoist yin and yang symbol represents nature's opposing but harmonious forces. It is also used in Confucianism.

This torii gate is a symbol of the Japanese religion of Shinto. Wooden torii gates mark the entrances to Shinto shrines.

This lotus flower is a Zen Buddhist symbol of purity and goodness. Zen is a type of Buddhism practiced in Japan.

ANCIENT RELIGIONS

FOR THE PEOPLES OF THE ANCIENT WORLD, THE GUIDING INFLUENCES ON their lives were the forces of nature. Rain was crucial for a good harvest, while steady winds and safe seas were vital for the success of trading expeditions. So people prayed to gods of nature, worshipping the sun, water and sky, and trying to please them with offerings and sacrifices.

▲ **This Mesopotamian statue of a winged bull** represents the guardian spirit that protected doorways.

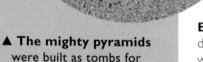

▲ **The mighty pyramids** were built as tombs for the early pharaohs of ancient Egypt. Their steep sides represented the rays of the sun, up which the pharaoh's soul was believed to walk to reach the sun god Ra.

Egypt and Mesopotamia

About 5,000 years ago, two of the world's greatest civilisations developed in the Near East. The Mesopotamians lived in modern-day Iraq, around the Tigris and Euphrates rivers, while ancient Egypt flourished along the River Nile. Both civilisations worshipped a large number of gods who they believed controlled all aspects of the universe, including life and death. The most important Egyptian god was the sun god, Ra. In Mesopotamia, the chief gods were Enlil, Lord of the Wind, and his father Anu, Lord of Heaven. It was important to obey the gods and not to make them angry.

▶ **The ancient Egyptians** had some 2,000 different gods and goddesses, whom they worshipped in temples and shrines. This picture shows, among others, Wadjet, the cobra goddess, and Hathor, goddess of beauty (standing, in red). The Egyptian ruler, or pharaoh, was also regarded as a god.

10

Cats were sacred to the goddess Bast, who represented the sun's healing power. Many cats were mummified when they died. Mummified mice were buried with the cat as food for its journey to the underworld. Anyone who killed a cat was sentenced to death.

Life after death

The ancient Egyptians were strong believers in life after death, and made careful burial preparations for life in the next world.

Each person had three souls – the *ka*, the *ba* and the *akh*. The souls would survive in the next world only if the dead person's body was preserved from decay. Because of this, dead bodies were "mummified". This involved giving the body a special treatment, called embalming, in order to preserve it.

First, the brain and other organs were removed and stored in containers called canopic jars. The body was packed in crystals of a chemical called natron salt

▶ The Mesopotamians built stepped towers, called ziggurats, where they worshipped the gods. The ziggurat at the city of Ur is thought to have been about 45 metres high. The priests climbed the steep stairs to make offerings at a shrine at the top.

to dry it out. It was then padded with sawdust and cloth, oiled and wrapped in strips of bandage. Finally, the body was placed in its coffin.

After death, a person's souls travelled to the underworld, where they undertook many trials and ordeals. The final test took place in the Judgement Hall of Osiris, god of the dead, where the person's heart was weighed against the Feather of Truth. If the heart tipped the scales, the person had led a sinful life and was fed to a monster. If the heart and the feather balanced, the person had led a good life and was allowed to enter the Kingdom of the West, a happy and carefree place.

◀ Many details of Mesopotamian religion were recorded on clay tablets. This "divinations" tablet was used to record predictions about the future. One such omen read: "If a man's chest-hair curls upward, he will become a slave."

Mesopotamian beliefs

The Mesopotamians believed that if their gods were not well looked after, they might become angry and send floods, plagues or war as a punishment.

To keep the gods happy, the Mesopotamians built magnificent temples as houses for the gods. Each day, priests and priestesses brought the gods offerings of food and drink. Special religious feast days were celebrated with music, dancing and the telling of stories about the gods' great deeds.

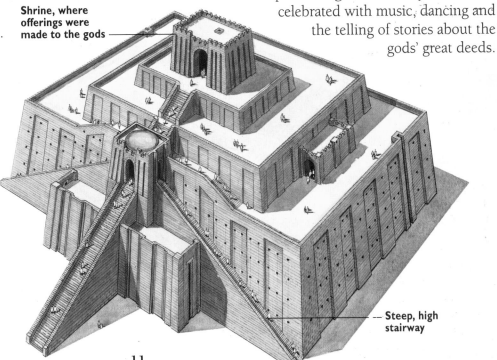

Shrine, where offerings were made to the gods

Steep, high stairway

Greece and Rome

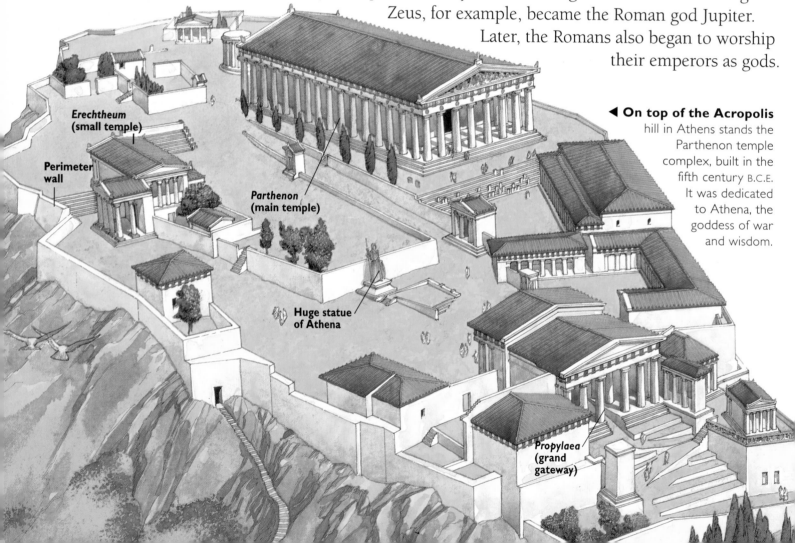

▲ Poseidon was the Greek god of the sea who lived in a fabulous underwater palace. He rode through the sea in a golden chariot pulled by white horses. He was also thought to cause earthquakes. The Romans called him Neptune.

The ancient Greeks (*c.*750–30 B.C.E.) believed that events on Earth were controlled by 12 gods called Olympians, led by Zeus, who lived on Mount Olympus in Greece. The gods behaved rather like humans, and showed many human emotions such as love, anger and jealousy. But they were also immortal and all-powerful, and worthy of honour and respect.

When the Romans conquered Greece in the second century B.C.E., they incorporated many of the Greek gods into their own religion. Zeus, for example, became the Roman god Jupiter. Later, the Romans also began to worship their emperors as gods.

◄ On top of the Acropolis hill in Athens stands the Parthenon temple complex, built in the fifth century B.C.E. It was dedicated to Athena, the goddess of war and wisdom.

Erechtheum (small temple)

Perimeter wall

Parthenon (main temple)

Huge statue of Athena

Propylaea (grand gateway)

Juno (Hera), goddess of women and marriage

Roman religion

In addition to worshipping the major gods and goddesses in Greek-style temples, every Roman family also worshipped its own guardian spirits, called the *Lares*, *Penates* and *Manes*. Each Roman house contained a shrine, or *Lararium*, to these gods.

The Romans were very superstitious. Before they did anything, such as embarking on a journey, they consulted the gods for advice. Priests called *haruspices* sacrificed animals and examined their innards for signs of the gods' will. Other priests called *augurs* looked for omens in the sky. If the gods disapproved, the journey would have to be cancelled.

Diana (Artemis), goddess of the moon and hunting

Temples and worship

The Greeks built beautiful temples as the gods' homes on Earth. Inside each temple stood a statue of the god or goddess to whom the temple was dedicated. Outside was a stone altar where animals and birds were sacrificed. The Greeks also had altars in their homes, where they said their daily prayers and made offerings of wine, called libations, to the gods.

Rites and festivals

Many festivals were held in honour of the Greek gods in order to gain their favour. One of the biggest festivals was the *Panathenaea* in Athens. It was celebrated every four years in honour of the goddess Athena, and festivities lasted for six days. On the final day of the festival, a huge procession of musicians, priests, soldiers and citizens made its way to the *Erechtheum* temple on the Acropolis. Here, a new dress was offered to the statue of the goddess.

Mars (Ares), god of war

◄ Roman religion adopted many of the Greek gods, although they were given different names. Here is a selection of Roman gods, with their original Greek names in brackets.

► A shrine of Roman household gods. In the centre stands the family's guardian spirit. The family began each day with prayers at the shrine.

Aztec and Inca gods

Until the fateful arrival of Spanish conquerors in the 16th century C.E., a number of great civilisations flourished in Central and South America. Among them were those of the Aztecs of Mexico and the Incas of Peru. Both had religions based on the worship of the sun and the forces of nature around them. The Aztecs and Incas believed that, although the gods governed everything, they could be influenced by offerings and sacrifices.

▲ **Quetzalcoatl** was the Aztec god of the wind and the Earth.

▶ **This Inca ritual knife,** made of turquoise and gold, was used to kill victims of sacrifice.

Nature gods

Both the Aztecs and Incas worshipped many gods. Farming was extremely important to both peoples, and many of the gods represented natural forces – such as the sun, rain and springtime – which either brought success or failure for crops. Prayers were said for good crops and good health.

The main Inca gods were Viracocha, the creator, and Inti, the sun god. The Incas also worshipped holy places called *huacas*, which included rocks, mountains, caves and rivers. The chief Aztec gods were Tonatiuh, god of the sun, and Tlaloc, the rain god. Some gods were depicted as animals. For example, Huitzilopochtli, the war god, appeared as a hummingbird. There were also three goddesses of maize (corn), the staple food of the Aztecs.

▶ **This carved Aztec stone** shows the sun, Tonatiuh, surrounded by symbols for the jaguar, wind, rain and water. They represent the four worlds, or "suns", thought to exist before this one.

Temples and sacrifice

The Aztecs and Incas built huge, pyramid-shaped temples in honour of the gods. These were the focus of many religious rites and ceremonies, as well as places of human sacrifice.

The Aztecs believed that the only way to fend off the coming destruction of the world was to feed the gods with human hearts and blood, and so keep them alive and well. The victims – often prisoners of war – were stretched over sacrificial stones while priests cut out their hearts. The victims' skulls were displayed in large racks outside the temples.

Norse myths

The Vikings, or Norsemen, were a seafaring people from Scandinavia who flourished in northern Europe from the 8th to 11th centuries C.E. The Vikings were brave adventurers, fierce warriors and successful traders. They had a rich mythology and told many tales of the exploits of their gods. By the end of the 11th century, most of the Vikings had converted to Christianity.

The Norse gods

The home of the Norse gods was Asgard, a kingdom that floated in the sky, separated from the Earth by a magical river. Asgard was ruled by the god Odin, who gave up the sight of one of his eyes to become all-knowing and all-powerful. Thor, the god of thunder and lightning, rode across the sky in his chariot, wielding his mighty hammer, Mjöllnir. Njord was the god of the sea and father of the twins Frey (god of fertility) and Freya (goddess of love and beauty).

The final battle

Many Norse gods were doomed to die in a bloody battle called Ragnarok. This would be the final struggle between good and evil – the Norse gods against their wicked enemies the giants – which would herald the end of the world. Some of the gods would survive to build a new and peaceful world.

▶ **Up-Helly-Aa** is a modern version of a Viking fire festival. It is celebrated each year in Lerwick, Shetland. A model Viking longboat is pulled through the town and set ablaze.

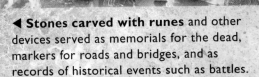

◀ **Stones carved with runes** and other devices served as memorials for the dead, markers for roads and bridges, and as records of historical events such as battles.

Judaism

Christianity **Islam**

▲ **Moses and his brother,** Aaron, were two of the great Jewish leaders.

PEOPLE OF THE BOOK

THREE OF THE WORLD'S GREAT RELIGIONS – JUDAISM, ISLAM AND CHRISTIANITY – are monotheistic religions, whose followers believe in one God. At the heart of each religion is a sacred book containing God's message for the world. These books are the Jewish Torah, *the Muslim* Qur'an *and the Christian* Bible.

Judaism

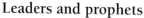

There are about 14 million Jews in the world today, living mainly in Israel, Europe and the United States. According to Jewish law, anyone whose mother is Jewish is a Jew. Many Jews actively follow Judaism as their religion.

Judaism began more than 4,000 years ago in the Middle East. The first Jews were members of a nomadic tribe called the Hebrews. They eventually settled in Canaan (now called Israel), which was the land promised to them by God. Here, they prospered under the rule of kings such as David and Solomon. King Solomon's Temple in Jerusalem became the early focus of their faith.

▲ **In C.E. 70,** the Romans destroyed the Second Temple of Jerusalem and carried off many of its sacred objects and treasures as loot.

Leaders and prophets

Judaism has no single founder, but many leaders and prophets (people who speak God's will). According to the Jewish scriptures, the first Jew was Abraham. It was he who taught the Hebrew people to worship one God, and entered into a covenant, or agreement, with God (*see page 18*).

The Jews settled in Canaan, but centuries later famine forced them to leave and go to Egypt in search of food. The Jews became slaves to the Egyptians, so God gave a man named Moses the task of leading them out of Egypt. After many years wandering in the deserts of Sinai, the Jews returned to Canaan, the Promised Land.

Sacred scriptures

The first five books of the Jewish Bible are known as the *Torah*. God gave them to Moses in the desert, on the top of Mount Sinai. The *Torah* is the most important of the Jewish scriptures, because it contains the laws that govern Jewish life. *Torah* means "teachings" in the Hebrew language. Copies of the *Torah* are handwritten on scrolls by specially trained scribes.

Interpretations, or explanations, of the laws by *rabbis* (experts in the *Torah*) are collected in the *Talmud* and other writings.

In addition to the *Torah*, the Jewish Bible also contains the books of the prophets, the Psalms (poems), proverbs (wise sayings), histories of the Jewish people and other holy writings. These scriptures also form the Old Testament of the Christian Bible (*see page 23*).

The Diaspora

Moses brought God's most important laws, the Ten Commandments, down from Mount Sinai carved on two stone tablets. The tablets were later kept in a golden box, called the Ark of the Covenant, inside King Solomon's Temple in Jerusalem.

In 586 B.C.E., the Babylonians burned down the Temple and took many Jewish people back to Babylon as captives. Fifty years later, the Jews returned from exile, led by a man named Ezra. He introduced reforms to make sure that the Jewish faith would survive. The Temple was rebuilt, but it was destroyed by the Romans in C.E. 70.

By C.E. 135, the Jews had been driven from their homeland and scattered all over the world. This is called the *Diaspora* ("Dispersion"). In the centuries that followed, the Jews settled in many different countries.

▲ **The Jewish scriptures** are written in Hebrew. This beautiful page is part of a decorated *Torah* produced in Germany in the Middle Ages.

▼ **The ancient city of Jerusalem** is a holy city not only for Jews, but also for Christians and Muslims.

Judaism
Beliefs and worship

The Jews worship one God, who created the world, is present everywhere and listens to their prayers. They believe that Jews have a special relationship with God, which dates from the time of Abraham. God made a covenant, or agreement, with Abraham, saying that if Abraham and his people worshipped God, their descendants would become God's Chosen People and live in the Promised Land of Canaan (now called Israel). Jews also believe in the Messiah, a leader who will be sent by God to bring peace and harmony to the world, and to rebuild the Temple. In daily life, Jews try to conduct their lives with love and respect for other people. The rules for daily life are set out in the *Torah*. They are called *mitzvot*, or commandments, and also form part of the Christian faith (*see pages 22–27*).

▲ **A father and son** studying the scriptures. Boys are allowed to read the *Torah* in the synagogue at the age of 13.

The Ten Commandments
The basis of the Jewish faith and the covenant between God and the Jewish people is summed up by the Ten Commandments:

1. *I am the Lord your God.*
2. *Worship no other god but me. Do not make images for yourselves to worship.*
3. *Do not misuse the name of the Lord your God.*
4. *Keep the Sabbath day holy.*
5. *Respect your father and mother.*
6. *Do not commit murder.*
7. *Do not commit adultery.*
8. *Do not steal.*
9. *Do not tell lies about others.*
10. *Do not envy other people's possessions.*

Symbolic Prayer Items

Tefillin (box of prayers worn on the head or arm)

Tallit (prayer shawl)

Yad (Silver reading finger for following the sacred texts)

Mezuzah (tiny case fixed to a door, containing a text from the *Torah*)

Kippah (skull cap)

Sefer-Torah (the twin scrolls of the *Torah*)

Menorah (seven-branched candlestick)

Replica of the Ten Commandments

Eternal Light

The Holy Ark

Torah

bbi's at

Reading table or bimah

◄ **All synagogues** have certain features in common. The Holy Ark, an alcove housing the *Torah*, is covered by an embroidered curtain. Above it burns the Eternal Light, which represents God's presence. Readings from the *Torah* are given from a central raised platform called a *bimah*.

The synagogue

The place where Jews can go to pray and listen to readings from the *Torah* is called the synagogue. It is also a centre for study, celebration and socialising (the word synagogue actually means "meeting place").

The *rabbi* leads the prayers and helps to guide people in how to keep the commandments. Large synagogues have services every day, but many Jews only go to the synagogue on special holy days.

Different groups

The main Jewish groups are Orthodox and Progressive Jews. Orthodox Jews believe that the *Torah* must be obeyed without question. In Orthodox synagogues, men and women worship separately, and services are held in Hebrew.

Progressive Jews believe that the ancient laws and practices should be interpreted in a way that makes them relevant to today's world. In Progressive synagogues, everyone sits together, and both Hebrew and the local language are used for prayers.

Judaism
Festivals and celebrations

The Sabbath (*Shabbat* in Hebrew) is the Jewish holy day. It lasts from sunset on Friday to nightfall on Saturday. It is a reminder that God created the world in six days, and rested on the seventh. The Sabbath is a day of rest, when no work should be done. It begins at home on Friday evening with the lighting of the Sabbath candles and a family meal. Many Jews visit the synagogue during the Sabbath.

Jewish law contains many rules about food. Strictly, all food should be *kosher*, or "clean". This means that meat and milk dishes may not be eaten together, or prepared using the same utensils. The *Torah* also forbids Jews to eat pork, shellfish and animals that have not been ritually slaughtered.

▲ **A *bar mitzvah* in Israel**. The boys are carrying the *Torah* scrolls from which they read during the ceremony.

▼ **The cornerstone** of Jewish life is the *Torah*. The *Torah* scrolls themselves are considered too sacred to touch, so the text is followed using a pointer called a *yad*.

▲ **Each item of Passover food** has a special meaning. Bitter herbs, for example, are a reminder of the misery of slavery, and eggs symbolise new life.

Festivals

During the year, there are many festivals to mark key events in the Jews' long history. One of the most important is *Pesach*, or Passover, which lasts for eight days during late March or early April. It celebrates the escape of the Jewish people from slavery in Egypt. The first evening of Passover is marked by a ceremony, called *Seder*, involving a special meal at which the Passover story is read from a book called the *Haggadah*.

Jewish New Year is celebrated in September or October with the festival of *Rosh Hashanah*. Ten days later comes *Yom Kippur*, or the Day of Atonement, which is spent in prayer, fasting and asking God's forgiveness for wrongdoings.

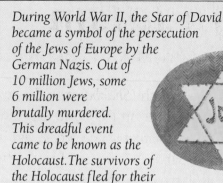

THE HOLOCAUST

During World War II, the Star of David became a symbol of the persecution of the Jews of Europe by the German Nazis. Out of 10 million Jews, some 6 million were brutally murdered. This dreadful event came to be known as the Holocaust. The survivors of the Holocaust fled for their lives. In 1948, the State of Israel was created so Jews could return to their historic homeland. Under a law called The Right to Return, Jews from all over the world can claim Israeli citizenship. Many have done so, although this has led to conflict with local Palestinian people and neighbouring Arab states.

Rites of passage

Major events in a Jew's own life are marked by special ceremonies. When boys reach the age of 13, they are considered old enough to take on religious responsibilities. This is marked by a ceremony in the synagogue called a *bar mitzvah* ("son of the commandments"), at which the boy reads from the Hebrew *Torah* and leads the prayers. Some synagogues have a similar ceremony for girls. It is called a *bat mitzvah* ("daughter of the commandments").

A Jewish wedding ceremony may take place at home or in a synagogue. The bride

▶ **In a Jewish wedding,** the bride and groom stand beneath the *chuppah* while the *rabbi* conducts the marriage ceremony.

and groom stand under a canopy called a *chuppah*, and exchange rings and vows. Then they sip from a glass of wine. The ceremony ends with the groom stamping on the wine glass, a reminder of the destruction of the Temple of Jerusalem.

Christianity

Christians are followers of Jesus Christ, a preacher and teacher who lived 2,000 years ago in Palestine, in the Middle East. (Today, most of Palestine is known as Israel.) In Jesus' time, Palestine was a mainly Jewish country and part of the Roman Empire.

Jesus was born and brought up a Jew, and gained many supporters among ordinary Jews. But the authorities were suspicious of him and plotted his downfall. In the centuries after Jesus' death, his disciples (followers) spread his message far and wide. Today, there are about 2,000 million Christians, living in every continent of the world.

◄ **The best-known** symbol of Christianity is the cross. It reminds Christians not only of how Jesus died, but also of how he rose again from the dead to save people from their sins (wrong actions against God and other people).

The life of Christ

Jesus was born in Bethlehem, where his mother, Mary, and father, Joseph, had travelled to take part in a Roman census. He was brought up in Nazareth, his parents' home town, where he studied Jewish scripture and probably trained to be a carpenter, like his father.

At the age of about 30, Jesus was baptised by his cousin, John, in the River Jordan. A new life had begun for him. For the next three years, Jesus travelled around the country teaching, preaching and healing the sick. His clear, simple message about God's love for all drew large crowds, but the religious leaders felt threatened by his popularity.

TEACHING BY PARABLES

To get his message across, Jesus told stories called parables. The parable of the Good Shepherd tells of a shepherd who had a hundred sheep. As he counted them into their pen one night, he discovered that one was missing. He went looking for the lost sheep immediately and was overjoyed to find it. By this, Jesus meant that God looks after everyone like a shepherd and is glad if even one person asks forgiveness for their sins and returns to God's "flock".

Death on the cross

In the last week of his life, Jesus went to Jerusalem for the Jewish feast of Passover. He was arrested while praying in the Garden of Gethsemane and charged with blasphemy. Pontius Pilate, the Roman governor, had him crucified (nailed to a cross and left to die).

Three days after his death, Jesus' disciples found his tomb empty. Over the next 40 days, Jesus appeared to them several times, before finally ascending (rising up) into heaven.

▼ **On the evening before his death,** Jesus shared the traditional Passover meal with his disciples. This meal is known as the Last Supper, and it is remembered in the ceremony of Holy Communion (see *page 25*).

The Holy Bible

The holy scriptures of Christianity are found in the Bible, a collection of 66 books. The Christian Bible is made up of the Old Testament, which contains the ancient Jewish scriptures, and the New Testament, which was written by Christians in the years after Jesus' death.

The New Testament contains four accounts of Jesus' teaching and life, known as gospels (meaning "good news"). It also records the acts of Jesus' disciples and includes letters written by Paul, one of the first leaders of the Christian Church. The Bible is the basis of Christian teaching, revealing not only God's will, but also how Christians should live their lives.

▲ **In the Middle Ages,** monks made beautiful handwritten copies of the Bible. This is a page from the Gospel of Mark.

Christianity

Beliefs and worship

Christians believe that Jesus was the Christ, or "anointed" one, and that, although he lived a human life, he was the Son of God – that is, God in human form. By giving up his own life, he paid the price for human sin. In rising again from the dead, he gave people the chance to know God and to experience God's love and forgiveness.

Christians believe in one God, but refer to three aspects of God: God the Father (creator of everything), God the Son (Jesus) and God the Holy Spirit (God's presence in the world). This is known as the Holy Trinity.

◀ **A Pentecostal service** in Britain. Pentecostalists emphasise the power of the Holy Spirit in people's lives. Worship is usually informal, emotional and spontaneous.

▶ **Some Christians** live as monks and nuns, taking vows of poverty, chastity and obedience in order to devote their lives to worshipping God.

Bell tower

Different Christian groups

Most Christians share the same basic beliefs, but there are many ways of expressing them. The three main groups within Christianity are Orthodox Christians, Roman Catholics and Protestants.
The Orthodox Church claims to follow the earliest traditions of Christianity begun by Jesus' disciples. More than half of all Christians belong to the Roman Catholic Church, which is led by the Pope in Rome. There are thousands of different Protestant churches, the first of which were founded in the 16th century, when some Christians broke away from the Roman Catholic Church.

Ways of worship

Christians worship God in private and in public, by praying at home or joining others for a Sunday service in a building called a church. Most church services are conducted by a priest or minister, and include hymns, prayers, Bible readings and a sermon or talk.

For most Christians, the centre of their worship is a ceremony called Communion. The worshippers eat a piece of bread (or wafer) and take a sip of grape juice or wine. This recalls the Last Supper, when Jesus blessed bread and wine, and shared it with his disciples, saying that the bread was his body and the wine was his blood, which he was sacrificing for people's lives. In this way, Christians remember Jesus' life and death, and celebrate his resurrection (rising from the dead).

Nave
Chancel
Organ pipes
Sanctuary lamp
Altar
Sanctuary
Aisle
Pulpit
Choir
Lectern
Transept
Porch
nt

◄ **Most churches** take aspects of their design and layout from the European cathedrals of the Middle Ages. The focus of a church is the altar, a large tablelike platform where Communion takes place. The person who is giving the sermon stands in the pulpit, while Bible readings are made from a lectern. There is also a font for baptisms.

Christianity
Festivals and celebrations

The most important Christian festivals remember events in Jesus' life, such as his birth, death, resurrection and ascension into heaven. Other festivals celebrate important events in a Christian's life, but these vary from place to place, and from church to church.

For all Christians, however, Sunday is a special day, because it is the day on which Jesus was raised from the dead. Like the Jewish Sabbath (*see page 20*), it is a day of rest on which no work should be done. Some Christians also celebrate the lives of the saints – people who are considered to have led very holy lives.

▲ **The priest talks** to the bride and groom at a wedding in the beautiful Cathedral of Seville, Spain. Christian brides traditionally wear white.

▶ **Infant baptism** involves making the sign of the cross in water on the foreheads of babies or small children. Some churches baptise adults by immersing them in water.

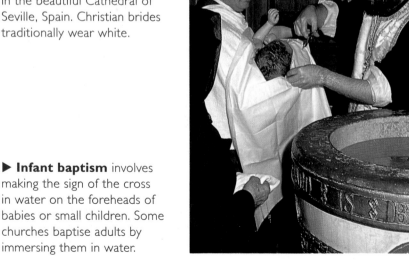

Times of life
Many Christians are baptised, or christened, as young children, to show that they will be taught about Jesus Christ. The water used symbolises a washing away of sin and the start of a new life as a Christian. Many young Christians later become full members of their church at a Confirmation ceremony. They confirm their faith in God and take Communion (*see page 25*).

A Christian wedding usually takes place in a church, before a minister or priest. The bride and groom ask God for his guidance and blessing. When a Christian dies, a funeral service is held in church. Prayers are said for the dead person, whose soul is believed to rise to heaven to enjoy everlasting life in God's presence.

Feasts and festivals

Christmas, which commemorates Jesus' birth, is one of the most important Christian festivals. The fourth Sunday before Christmas marks the beginning of Advent, a time when Christians look forward to celebrating Jesus' birthday. Christmas traditionally occurs on 25 December, although no one really knows when Jesus was born. Twelve days after Christmas, on 6 January, comes Epiphany, which remembers the visit of three wise men to the infant Jesus.

Lent is the period before Easter when Christians remember their sins. It commemorates the 40 days and nights Jesus spent fasting and praying in the desert, before he started preaching his message.

Holy Week, the week before Easter, falls in late March or early April. On Good Friday, Christians remember the day on which Jesus died. It is called "good" because it shows Jesus' goodness in dying to save others. Easter Sunday is the most important Christian festival, when Christians attend church to celebrate Jesus' rising from the dead. Many people give each other Easter eggs (a symbol of new life).

The Feast of the Ascension takes place on a Thursday, 40 days after Easter Sunday. It marks the day on which Jesus went up into heaven. It is followed by Pentecost, which is a celebration of the giving of the Holy Spirit to Jesus' disciples.

▲ **On 12 December,** a festival takes place in Mexico called Our Lady of Guadalupe. It is held in honour of Christ's mother, Mary, the patron saint of Mexico.

◄ **In many Christian homes,** an Advent candle is lit and a prayer is said on each of the four Sundays before Christmas. On Christmas Day, a large red candle is added to represent Jesus' birth.

Islam

About 1,400 years ago in the city of Mecca, in western Arabia (now Saudi Arabia), the Prophet Muhammad began proclaiming the message of Islam – that there is only one God (or in Arabic, Allah). Muslims, the followers of Islam, believe that Muhammad was the last in a series of prophets through whom Allah revealed his wishes for the world. The word "Islam" comes from the Arabic for "submission". Muslims are people who submit to (obey) Allah's will and try to live in a way that is pleasing to Allah.

▲ **Islamic buildings** are beautifully decorated with geometric patterns and shapes. Human figures are not allowed to be shown.

▼ **Islam was brought** to China in the eighth century C.E. by Muslim traders. Green is the colour of Islam. It is used on flags and banners in many Islamic countries.

The spread of Islam

After Muhammad's death, Islam spread rapidly through Arabia and its neighbouring countries. In the seventh and eighth centuries C.E., Muslim armies established a vast Islamic empire, stretching from Spain and North Africa to India. Muslim traders spread the faith even farther afield. Today, more than 20 percent of the world's people are Muslims, living in over 120 different countries.

◀ **As Islam spread,** so did the influence of Islamic art, architecture, science and culture. Chess was brought to Europe by the Muslims in the 10th century C.E. It came originally from India.

▶ **This beautiful mosaic** adorns the entrance to a mosque in the ancient city of Samarkand, Uzbekistan, which was a great centre of Islamic culture in the 14th century.

▼ **Learning the *Qur'an*** is a vital part of a Muslim's education. Most Muslims try to read it in its original Arabic, even if Arabic is not their own language.

The life of Muhammad

Muhammad was born in Mecca in about 570 C.E. At the age of 25, he married a wealthy widow named Khadija. Although he grew rich and successful, he was unhappy with life and dismayed by the greed he saw around him. Muhammad spent more and more time in meditation and contemplation. Then, one night, as he lay asleep on Mount Hira, an angel appeared and began to reveal God's message to him. Many more revelations followed.

Muhammad returned to Mecca and urged people to stop worshipping idols and to worship Allah, the one true God, instead. Not everyone welcomed his message, and in 622 C.E. he was forced to flee to the city of Medina, where he gained many followers. Seven years later, Muhammad returned in triumph to Mecca. He died in Medina in 632.

The Qur'an

The holy book of the Muslims is called the *Qur'an*, which means "recitation". It is believed to contain the words of Allah, as revealed to Muhammad. The *Qur'an* tells Muslims how to worship, how to treat other people, what to eat and wear, and how to live a good life. Muslims believe that the *Qur'an* has always existed in heaven, written in Arabic on a tablet of stone.

Islam
Beliefs and worship

Wherever they live in the world, Muslims share the same set of beliefs. These central beliefs are known as the Five Pillars of Islam. The first pillar is *shahada*, a statement of faith that says: "There is no god but Allah and Muhammad is his prophet." The second pillar is *salat*, or prayer. The giving of alms to the poor and needy is the third pillar, called *zakat*. The fourth pillar, *sawm*, requires Muslims to fast during the holy month of *Ramadan* (*see page 32*). The fifth and final pillar is *Hajj*, the name given to the pilgrimage to Mecca which all Muslims hope to perform at least once during their lifetime (*see page 33*).

Minaret (the call to prayer is made from here)

▼ **Some mosques** are large and highly ornate, while others are very simple structures. The first mosque was built by Muhammad and his followers in Medina. It was a modest wooden building with a roof of thatched palm leaves.

Sahn (courtyard)

Riwags (shady arcades)

Fauwara (fountains)

▶ **The Sufis are Muslims** who use dance, music and chanting to reach out to Allah. Among the most famous Sufis are the Whirling Dervishes from Turkey, who perform spectacular spinning dances.

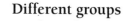

Different groups

Within Islam there are two main groups – the Sunnis and the Shi'ites. Both of these groups accept the teachings of Islam, but they disagree about who was the rightful leader (or *caliph*) of the Muslims after the death of Muhammad in 632 C.E. The Sunni group is larger; its members make up about 80 percent of the world's Muslims.

The mosque

Muslims can offer prayers to Allah anywhere, provided that they choose a clean place or lay a prayer mat on the floor. Many prefer to worship in buildings called mosques. Outside each mosque is a tall tower, or *minaret*, from which a man known as a *muezzin* calls the faithful to prayer.

The *minaret* looks down upon a spacious courtyard, or *sahn*, which is surrounded by shady arcades called *riwags*. Inside the courtyard are fountains (*fauwara*), whose waters symbolise purity. Worshippers can bathe in the fountains before entering the mosque. Leading off from the courtyard is the *zulla*, or prayer hall.

Mihrab (showing direction of Mecca)

Zulla (prayer hall)

Maqsura (ornate wooden screen)

Minbar (pulpit)

▲ **This glimpse inside** the exquisite Tillya Kari mosque in Samarkand, Uzbekistan, shows the *mihrab* arch, which is decorated with verses from the *Qur'an*.

▲ **Although mosques differ** in size and appearance, most have several features in common, such as the *minaret*, *mihrab* and *minbar*.

Visiting the mosque

Inside a mosque, men and women worship separately. They must always face Mecca to pray. The worshippers gather in the prayer hall, where the direction of Mecca is indicated by an empty arch, called the *mihrab*, in one of the walls. Beside the *mihrab* is a pulpit called the *minbar*, from which the *imam* (prayer-leader) gives the sermon and leads the prayers.

Prayer – the second pillar

Muslims are expected to pray five time a day – at sunrise, noon, mid-afternoon, sunset and at night. Muslims pray in Arabic, following a fixed order of movements and words. First, they make sure they are facing toward Mecca, then they bow, kneel and touch the floor with their foreheads and noses. Finally, they sit back on their heels.

Friday is the Muslim holy day, the only day on which men must go to the mosque to pray. Women may also attend Friday prayers, but it is not compulsory. Many women say their prayers at home instead.

Islam
Festivals and celebrations

There are many fasts and festivals throughout the Muslim year. The most important is the holy month of *Ramadan*, which commemorates Allah's first revelations to Muhammad. During *Ramadan*, Muslims fast – that is, have nothing to eat or drink – from dawn to dusk. They believe that the practice of fasting teaches self-discipline. It also reminds them of the world's poor and hungry, and makes them more aware of Allah's blessings.

Ramadan ends with the sighting of the new moon in the sky. Muslims celebrate the end of their fast with the festival of *Id ul-Fitr*, when they visit the mosque, call on friends and relatives, and eat a feast of special foods. Muslims are not allowed to eat pork or drink alcohol.

Times of life
Special prayers and ceremonies accompany every stage of a Muslim's life. As soon as a baby is born, prayers are whispered into its ears. These prayers are the very first words the baby hears. Seven days later comes its *aqiqah*, or naming ceremony.

Family life is very important, and the *Qur'an* encourages Muslims to marry. Divorce is allowed, but married couples must try hard to solve their differences first.

When Muslims die, they are buried, not cremated. They believe the dead body must be respected and not harmed in any way.

▲ A funeral procession
in Pakistan, during which the mourners say prayers and recite verses from the *Qur'an*. The dead person is always buried with his or her head facing toward Mecca.

32

◄ **To celebrate the festival** of *Id ul-Fitr*, Muslims exchange cards to wish each other "*Id Mubarak*" or "Happy Id". Inside the card is a prayer or a verse from the *Qur'an*.

WOMEN IN ISLAM

Throughout the Muslim world, the role of women is changing. Sometimes this leads to clashes between traditional and modern attitudes. In some Islamic countries, such as Saudi Arabia, women lead very strict lives. They have to wear traditional robes and veils that cover their whole bodies, in keeping with the Qur'an's requirement that they should dress modestly. They are not allowed to work, or even to drive cars. In countries with more relaxed rules, such as Syria, women can wear Western-style dress, although some still follow tradition. Syrian women are actively encouraged to study and work.

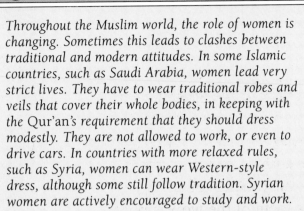

Pilgrimage to Mecca

All Muslims try to make the *Hajj* (the pilgrimage to Mecca) at least once in their lives, to worship at the *Ka'aba*. The *Ka'aba* is a cube-shaped shrine believed to have been built by Abraham, one of the prophets of Islam, and Ishmael, one of his sons.

The pilgrims walk seven times, anticlockwise, around the *Ka'aba*. Then they walk or run seven times between two nearby hills. Next comes a 26-km walk to Mount Arafat, where Muhammad preached his last sermon. On the way back to Mecca, they throw stones at three stone pillars, which represent Satan, before making a final seven circuits of the *Ka'aba*. The *Hajj* ends with the festival of *Id ul-Adha* and the sacrifice of a sheep or goat.

◄ **The *Ka'aba*** in Mecca is visited by more than 2 million Muslims each year. Before pilgrims begin the *Hajj*, they change into plain, identical clothes to show that they are all equal in Allah's eyes.

Hinduism

Jainism

Sikhism

Zoroastrianism

Buddhism

▲ **Hindus consider cows** to be sacred animals, so they never eat beef. Many Hindus are vegetarians, believing in nonviolence toward living things.

RELIGIONS OF INDIA

INDIA IS A MELTING POT OF RELIGIONS. FOUR OF THE WORLD'S MAJOR FAITHS began here – Hinduism, Buddhism, Jainism and Sikhism. Many other religions are practiced in India, although their origins lie elsewhere. They include Islam, Christianity, Judaism and Zoroastrianism.

Hinduism

Hinduism is one of the world's oldest and most varied religions, with some 700 million followers called Hindus. The word "Hinduism" is not a word that Hindus use to describe their own religion. They call it *sanatana dharma*, meaning "the eternal law".

No one is sure exactly when Hinduism began, but its roots stretch back more than 4,000 years to the time of the great Indus Valley Civilisation in the west Indian subcontinent. Archaeologists have found clay statues showing gods and goddesses similar to those worshipped by Hindus today. In around 1500 B.C.E., the nomadic Aryan people invaded northwest India. Their religious ideas mixed with those of the people of the Indus Valley to form the basis of Hinduism as it is practiced today.

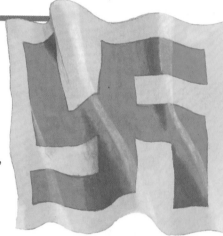

▲ **The swastika** is an ancient Hindu sign of peace and good luck. It literally means "It is well." Sadly, the German Nazis used a twisted swastika as their symbol during World War II, turning it into a symbol of evil. To Hindus, it has exactly the opposite meaning.

◀ **Pilgrims flock** to the city of Varanasi in northern India to bathe in the sacred River Ganges. They believe that this will help to wash away their sins.

The main Hindu gods

Most Hindus believe in a supreme soul or spirit, without shape or form, called Brahman. The many Hindu gods and goddesses represent the different aspects of Brahman's power and character. The three main gods are Brahma (the creator), Vishnu (the preserver or protector) and Shiva (the destroyer). Hindus may worship one god, many gods or none at all. Most Hindus find it helps to have a picture or statue of a god to focus on while they pray. Vishnu and Shiva are extremely popular, with temples and followers all over India.

Shiva

Brahma

Vishnu

◀ **Statues and paintings** of Hindu gods and goddesses often have a deeper meaning than first meets the eye. The deities are often shown with several arms, hands or heads to indicate their special qualities or powers. Brahma, for example, has four faces to show that his rule extends to all four corners of the Earth.

ॐ THE CASTE SYSTEM ॐ

Since Aryan times, Hindu society has been divided into four classes, or castes, depending on what jobs people did. The higher castes are the Brahmins (priests), Kshatriyas (nobles and soldiers) and Vaishyas (merchants). Below them are Shudras (labourers). Outside the caste system are the people with the lowliest jobs, such as leather tanners and cleaners.

Other Hindu deities

In addition to the three main gods, Hindus worship hundreds of other gods and goddesses. Some are worshipped throughout India, while others are popular in just one particular region or village. Some families have their own special family gods that they have worshipped for generations.

Two of the most popular deities are Rama and Krishna. Both are incarnations of the god Vishnu. Vishnu appeared on Earth many times to save the world from disaster, but he was always in disguise. These incarnations are known as *avatars*.

Hindu deities are often a mixture of good and evil, kindness and cruelty. For example, Parvati, the wife of Shiva, is worshipped both as the kindly Mother Goddess and the terrible, blood-thirsty Durga, goddess of war.

Another much-loved god is Ganesha, the elephant-headed son of Shiva and Parvati. Ganesha protects travellers and removes obstacles from people's lives. Hindus pray to this god when something new happens, like moving to a new house.

Hinduism
Beliefs and worship

There are no set rules for being a Hindu, but most Hindus share the same basic beliefs. They believe that when you die, your soul is reborn in another body, as a person or an animal. This cycle of birth and rebirth is called *samsara*. The aim of every Hindu's life is to break free of the cycle and gain *moksha*, or salvation, in which the soul merges with Brahman. How you are reborn depends on your actions in your previous life. This process is called *karma*. If you led a good life, you will have a better rebirth and move closer to *moksha*.

▲ Outside most temples are stalls selling different types of *prasad* (gifts) for worshippers to offer to the deity inside.

▶ A Hindu temple in India. A statue of the deity to which the temple is dedicated is kept in the holiest part of the temple (the *garbhagriha*), which lies beneath a towering roof called the *sikhara*. The temple is surrounded at its four corners by smaller shrines.

Sikhara (roof)

Garbhagriha (inner chamber, containing image of deity)

Terrace

Staircase

Ardhamandapa (entrance porch)

◀ An extract from the *Brihad-Aranyaka Upanishad*, which is written in Sanskrit, the sacred language of India. It says:

*"From the unreal lead me to truth,
From darkness lead me to light,
From death lead me to immortality."*

ॐ
असतो मा
सद्गमय।
तमसो मा
ज्योतिर्गमय।
मृत्योर्मा
मृतं गमय॥

Places of worship

Many Hindus worship in temples. Each temple, or *mandir*, is dedicated to a particular god or goddess, and is believed to be the deity's earthly home. A statue of the deity is kept in a shrine in the innermost, holiest part of the temple.

Hindus can visit the temple to worship whenever they like, because there are no set services. Some people go every day, while others only visit on special occasions such as festival days.

In addition to large temples, there are also small shrines on many street corners. Most Hindus also worship at home, setting aside a special place as a shrine. The shrine may simply be a picture or statue of a deity.

Visiting the temple

Hindus always take off their shoes before entering a temple, and women cover their heads as a sign of respect. Hindus visit a temple not simply to pray, but also to have a *darshana* (viewing) of the statue representing the deity. They take offerings of fruit, flowers and incense. These gifts are called *prasad*. The priest presents the gifts to the deity to be blessed. He returns them to the worshippers, and marks their foreheads with a red mark of blessing, called a *tilaka*. This ceremony is known as *puja*.

Afterward, they walk clockwise around the inner shrine, with their right hands toward the deity. Hindus eat with their right hands, and consider them to be clean and pure.

▲ *Sadhus* are Hindu holy men who give up their homes and possessions to live a life of meditation and prayer. Other worshippers give them food and money.

Sacred texts

The oldest Hindu sacred texts are four collections of hymns, prayers and magic spells, called the *Vedas*, which were composed over 3,000 years ago. Other important texts include the *Upanishads*, and two long poems, the *Mahabharata* and the *Ramayana*.

The *Upanishads* are teachings presented in the form of stories and parables told by *gurus* (teachers) to their pupils. The *Mahabharata* tells of a war between two royal families, the Kauravas and Pandavas, while the *Ramayana* tells how the god Rama rescued his wife, Sita, from Ravana, the evil demon king.

—Smaller shrine

▲ **In this scene** from the *Bhagavad Gita*, the most important part of the *Mahabharata*, Arjuna, one of the Pandavas, shoots off the head of his enemy, Karna, with an arrow. His chariot is driven by the god Krishna (shown with blue skin).

Hinduism
Festivals and celebrations

Almost every day, a festival is being celebrated somewhere in India. There are thousands of Hindu festivals, large and small, to mark special occasions such as the birthdays of the gods and goddesses, harvest time and family events. No one can possibly celebrate them all! Many Hindus also make pilgrimages to sacred places, such as the city of Varanasi, on the banks of the holy River Ganges.

▲ **A boy wearing traditional clothes,** ready to attend a relative's wedding. The bride will wear a beautiful silk *sari.*

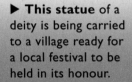

▶ **This statue** of a deity is being carried to a village ready for a local festival to be held in its honour.

Celebrations of life

Samskaras are ceremonies to mark major events in a Hindu's life. Ten days after a baby's birth, a naming ceremony is held, and the baby's horoscope is drawn up by a priest. Later in life, it will be used to set a favourable wedding date.

At the age of 9 or 10, a boy from the top three castes, or classes, is given a sacred thread (a long loop of cotton) to wear. This ceremony marks the start of his adult life.

Hindu weddings involve several days of joyful rituals, ceremonies and feasting. When Hindus die, their bodies are cremated so that the sacred fire can carry their souls heavenward to be reborn.

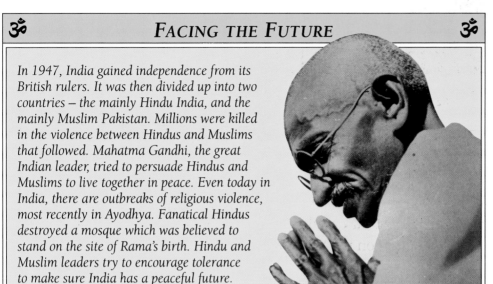

In 1947, India gained independence from its British rulers. It was then divided up into two countries – the mainly Hindu India, and the mainly Muslim Pakistan. Millions were killed in the violence between Hindus and Muslims that followed. Mahatma Gandhi, the great Indian leader, tried to persuade Hindus and Muslims to live together in peace. Even today in India, there are outbreaks of religious violence, most recently in Ayodhya. Fanatical Hindus destroyed a mosque which was believed to stand on the site of Rama's birth. Hindu and Muslim leaders try to encourage tolerance to make sure India has a peaceful future.

Festivals

Most Hindus celebrate the main festivals of the year – *Diwali*, *Holi* and *Dussehra*. These are lively, colourful occasions. People visit the temple, eat special food and exchange sweets and gifts. *Diwali* is the festival of lights, celebrated in late October or early November. During *Holi*, which marks the coming of spring in March or April, people light bonfires and shower each other with coloured water and powders. *Dussehra*, held in September, marks Rama's triumph over the evil Ravana (*see page 37*).

▼ **During Diwali,** people place lamps outside their doors to guide Rama home after his long years of exile. Diwali is also the time for worshipping Lakshmi, the goddess of good fortune.

▲ **Every 12 years,** in January or February, millions of pilgrims flock to the banks of the River Ganges at Allahabad, to celebrate the *Kumbha Mela*, a great bathing fair.

Jainism

The most important figure in the Jain religion is Mahavira ("Great Hero"), who lived in India in the 6th century B.C.E. Born into the *Kshatriya* warrior caste (*see page 35*), he left home when he was 30 to become a monk. For 12 years he led a life of fasting and meditation. Eventually, he freed himself from worldly cares and gained enlightenment, becoming a *Jina,* or Conqueror.

Mahavira spent the rest of his life preaching and teaching. By the time of his death at the age of 72, he had gained many followers across western India. Today there are some 3.5 million Jains, most of whom live in India.

▲ Devout Jains sweep the ground in front of them to avoid stepping on insects and wear masks to avoid swallowing them.

Jain beliefs

Jains do not believe in a god, but worship 24 spiritual teachers, called *Tirthankaras*, and use them as guides in their daily lives. Mahavira was the 24th and greatest *Tirthankara.*

Like Hindus and Buddhists, Jains believe in the rebirth of the soul (*see page 36*). By basing their lives on "right faith, right conduct and right knowledge" (the Three Jewels, or *Triratna*), they hope to break free of the cycle of birth and rebirth and gain salvation.

Jain monks and nuns devote their lives to meditation and studying the scriptures. They promise to keep five "great vows" of chastity, poverty, telling the truth, not stealing and nonviolence.

Respect for life

One of the central beliefs of the Jain religion is *ahimsa*, or nonviolence. Jains believe that every living thing, no matter how small, has a soul and should not be harmed. For this reason, Jains are strict vegetarians, and fasting plays an important part in Jain life.

Jain temples

Each Jain temple contains statues of the 24 *Tirthankaras*, on which a worshipper focuses during prayer. The worshipper stands in front of the statues and bows to them. Next, he or she pours an offering of the "five nectars" – diluted milk, yoghurt, butter, sugar and flowers – over the statues. Pure water is then used to wash the statues clean.

▼ **Every 12 to 14 years,** this huge statue of the Jain saint, Lord Bahubali, is covered with offerings as part of a great festival.

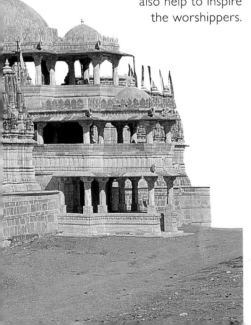

◄ **The outsides of Jain temples** are very beautiful, to show the holiness of the sacred images inside. The beautiful buildings also help to inspire the worshippers.

Zoroastrianism

The roots of Zoroastrianism stretch back more than 3,000 years to ancient Persia and the prophet Zoroaster (or Zarathustra). The peaceful society in which Zoroaster lived was being torn apart by warlike tribes, and it was this struggle between good and evil that inspired his teachings.

There are about 100,000 Zoroastrians in the world today. Many live in west India and are known as Parsis (from the word "Persia"). Their ancestors fled from Iran in the ninth century C.E., when Iran became a Muslim country.

▲ **Zoroaster** is shown here carrying a staff and a fire symbol. His teachings form the *Avesta* (the Zoroastrian scriptures). For centuries, they were thought too sacred to be written down and were passed on by word of mouth.

Main beliefs

Zoroastrians believe in one God, called Ahura Mazda, who created the world and everything in it. His enemy is the evil spirit Angra Mainyu, who will eventually be defeated by the forces of good. There are also six lesser gods, called the Amesha Spentas.

When people die, they are judged according to how good or evil they have been during their lives. If the good deeds outweigh the bad, they are allowed to pass over a bridge and enter heaven. But if the bad deeds outweigh the good, they fall off the bridge and plummet into hell.

Zoroaster also taught that one day a saviour will come who will banish all evil and return the world to a state of perfection.

▲ **Zoroastrians worship** in fire temples. This one is in Bombay, India. All Zoroastrians share the belief that they should live good lives in order to bring about the salvation of the world.

SACRED FIRE

At the heart of Zoroastrian worship is the sacred fire, which represents righteousness and truth. The fire is kept burning at the fire altar in the temple, which is tended by priests. Zoroastrians pray before a source of light five times a day. At home this is usually a lamp instead of a fire. As they pray, they tie and untie their kustis, sacred woollen belts which bind them to their religion and community. A white undershirt, called a sudreh, is worn at all times and symbolises purity. When a person dies, the kusti and sudreh are laid on top of the body on a white sheet.

Rites and rituals

On special occasions such as weddings, deaths and the days on which boys receive their sacred belts, the priests hold ceremonies in the fire temple. Ordinary people are not allowed to attend these ceremonies, but they can go to other services of thanksgiving and worship that celebrate festivals and events in their history. These can be held in any clean place.

▼ **Zoroastrians do not cremate** or bury their dead, because they believe that this would pollute the Earth. Instead, they place the dead bodies in circular stone towers, called Towers of Silence, for birds of prey to eat.

Buddhism

The founder of Buddhism was Siddhartha Gautama, a royal prince born in Nepal in about 563 B.C.E. After many years of prayer and meditation, Siddhartha gained enlightenment, meaning that he finally understood the basic truths of life. He was given the title of Buddha ("awakened one").

The Buddha did not want to be worshipped as a god. He taught that people would be happier if they took responsibility for their own thoughts and actions. His teachings were simply a guide for living.

Today there are more than 400 million Buddhists. Most live in Asia, although the peaceful, caring ideals of Buddhism have also attracted many followers in Western countries.

The life of the Buddha

Although Siddhartha grew up in his father's luxurious palace, shielded from the outside world, he was unhappy. Finally, he left the palace on a journey that changed his life.

First he saw an old man, then a sick man, then a dead man. Life was full of such suffering, he was told. Last, he saw a poor monk, who had no possessions and yet was still very contented. Siddhartha vowed to be like the monk, and left the palace behind forever.

Many years of fasting and prayer later, he sat under a tree in Bodh Gaya, India. He closed his eyes and began to meditate. When he opened his eyes, he knew he had at last seen the truth and found a way out of suffering.

◄ **The lotus plant** is an important Buddhist symbol. Its flowers turn toward the sun, just as the followers of the Buddha turn toward knowledge. Lotus flowers are also sacred to Hindus.

◄ **This statue of the Buddha** is in Anuradhapura, Sri Lanka. After his enlightenment, the Buddha spent the rest of his life travelling around India, teaching and preaching. He soon had a loyal band of followers.

▶ **The Buddha died,** aged 80, in the town of Kushinagara, India, lying on his side, as shown by this statue. He then entered *Nirvana*, the blissful state seen by Buddhists as the end to all suffering.

What the Buddha taught

The Buddha's enlightenment had shown him that people suffered because they were never happy with what they had and always wanted more. They needed to learn new ways of thinking and behaving. The Buddha set out his basic teachings in his first sermon. At the centre of his sermon were the Four Noble Truths:

1. *Human life is full of suffering.*
2. *The cause of suffering is greed.*
3. *There is an end to suffering.*
4. *The way to end suffering is to follow the Middle Path.*

The Middle Path lay between extreme luxury and extreme hardship. It had eight steps that would lead people to live wiser and more compassionate lives:

1. *Right understanding (of the Buddha's teachings).*
2. *Right attitude (positive thinking).*
3. *Right speech (not telling lies).*
4. *Right action (helping others).*
5. *Right work (doing a useful job).*
6. *Right effort (doing good things).*
7. *Right mindfulness (thinking before you speak or act).*
8. *Right meditation (developing a calm, happy mind).*

▲ **Buddhists believe**
that people are reborn many times before they reach *Nirvana*. In this painting of the Wheel of Life (the symbol of the Buddha's teaching), many different states of rebirth are shown.

Buddhism
Buddhism in practice

Some time after the Buddha's death, his followers split into different groups, or "schools", depending on how they interpreted his teachings. The Mahayana School spread from India to Nepal, Vietnam, China, Korea and Japan (you can read about Japanese Buddhism on *pages 56–57*). The Theravada School spread to Sri Lanka, Myanmar, Thailand, Cambodia and Laos, while the Vajrayana School reached Tibet, Bhutan and Mongolia. In daily life, all Buddhists follow a set of guidelines called the Five Precepts. The guidelines are: do not harm or kill living things; do not take things unless they are freely given; lead a decent life; do not speak unkindly or tell lies; and do not take drugs or drink alcohol.

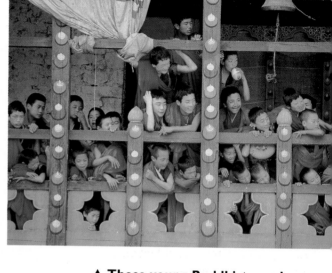

▲ **These young Buddhist monks** in Bhutan are crowding excitedly on to a wooden balcony to watch a festival procession go by.

Shrines and stupas

For Buddhists, the Middle Path (*see page 45*) is a complete way of life that they try to follow closely at all times. Buddhists visit shrines and temples to pay their respects to the Buddha and to meditate with other Buddhists. Some Buddhists have shrines in their homes. The first Buddhist shrines were 10 dome-shaped mounds, or *stupas*, which were built to contain the Buddha's ashes (his burnt remains). More *stupas* were built to house other holy relics, such as copies of sacred texts and the ashes of important monks. Eventually, *stupas* became elaborate buildings. Many now form part of larger temple complexes, where Buddhists go to pray.

▶ **This is one of oldest surviving *stupas*,** in Sanchi, India. As Buddhism spread from India to other countries, different styles of *stupa* developed. In Sri Lanka, they are bell shaped, while Tibetan *stupas* are taller and set on a number of platforms. Japanese and Chinese *stupas* are tiered towers.

The life of a monk

Together, Buddhist monks and nuns are known as the *sangha*. The *sangha* is one of the Three Jewels of Buddhism – three things that are treasured because they give people help and support. The other two Jewels are the Buddha himself and the *dharma,* his teaching.

The Buddha lived for many years as a wandering monk, relying on gifts of food to sustain him. Today, monks live simple, strict lives, studying sacred texts and learning to meditate. In some countries, such as Myanmar and Thailand, young boys spend several months in a monastery as part of their education. Some choose to stay on, taking vows and becoming monks themselves.

Since the Chinese army invaded Tibet in 1959, hundreds of Buddhist monasteries have been destroyed and thousands of monks arrested or killed. The Dalai Lama, the spiritual leader of Tibetan Buddhists, now lives in exile in Dharamsala, India, with thousands of his followers. His travels around the world publicise his country's plight. Visitors flock to Dharamsala to study, hoping that they will also be granted an audience with the Dalai Lama himself.

▶ **These Tibetan monks** from the *Gelukpa* ("Yellow Hat") sect are blowing special ceremonial long horns. The Dalai Lama is the leader of the Yellow Hats. *Lama* is the Tibetan word for a spiritual teacher.

Sikhism

The Sikh religion began about 500 years ago in Punjab, northwestern India. The two main religions in India at that time were Hinduism and Islam, but there were deep divisions between the two, and many people felt excluded from them. Guru Nanak, a religious teacher, introduced the new religion of Sikhism, which taught tolerance of other faiths. When Guru Nanak died, his teaching was carried on by nine other "gurus", or teachers, ending with Guru Gobind Singh.

There are about 16 million Sikhs in the world today, most of whom still live in Punjab. There are also large Sikh communities in Britain and the United States.

▲ **The person** who looks after and reads from the *Guru Granth Sahib* is called a *granthi*, or reader. The *granthi*, who can be a man or a woman, is chosen from among the most devout worshippers.

What Sikhs believe

Sikhs believe that there is only one God, and they try to remember God in everything they do. This task of remembering is called *simran* and is closely linked to the idea of *seva*, or "service". *Seva* involves doing things for others without thinking of your own reward. By practising these two ideals and following the example set by the gurus, Sikhs hope to grow closer to God.

Guru Nanak preached that, in God's eyes, everyone is equal. To show this, all Sikh men take the surname *Singh* (meaning "Lion"), and all Sikh women take the surname *Kaur* (meaning "Princess").

◀ **Guru Nanak** (*centre*) and the other nine Sikh gurus, with haloes to show their holiness. Also in the picture are a Hindu and a Muslim, both companions of Guru Nanak.

Ways of worship

Many Sikhs visit a *gurudwara*, or temple, to pray. The word *gurudwara* means "the gateway of the guru".

When entering the temple, worshippers must take off their shoes and cover their heads as a mark of respect. They bow in front of the Sikh holy book, the *Guru Granth Sahib*, and sit to listen to hymns read from the scriptures.

After the final prayer, called the *Ardas*, the worshippers share *karah prasad*, a food offering which is made of sweet semolina mixed with water and butter.

▼ **The Golden Temple** in Amritsar, Punjab, is the holiest Sikh shrine. It was built on the site where Guru Nanak once meditated.

Sacred text

When Guru Gobind Singh died in 1708, he told the Sikhs that in the future the sacred scriptures should be their new guru. The scriptures, collected together in the *Guru Granth Sahib*, are devotional hymns composed by six of the gurus and other holy men.

In the *gurudwara*, the *Guru Granth Sahib* is wrapped in silk and kept under a special canopy. The *Guru Granth Sahib* is read during services and on occasions such as weddings and naming ceremonies. To name a child, the reader opens the *Guru Granth Sahib* at random and calls out a word. The name chosen for the child must begin with the same initial letter as that word.

THE FIVE KS

Devout Sikhs have five symbols of their faith. They are known as the five Ks, because each begins with the letter K in the Punjabi language.

Kesh (uncut hair) symbolises obedience to God's will

Kangha (wooden comb) symbolises cleanliness

Kachh (shorts, worn under other clothes) symbolise goodness

Kara (steel bracelet, worn on right wrist) symbolises eternity

Kirpan (sword) symbolises strength

Confucianism

Taoism

Shinto

Zen Buddhism

▲ **Confucius is remembered** for his wise sayings, such as: "A good person always seeks to help others to do good, not to do ill."

CHINESE AND JAPANESE RELIGIONS

A VARIETY OF RELIGIOUS BELIEFS ARE PRACTISED IN CHINA AND JAPAN. Confucianism and Taoism originated in China, and Shinto in Japan. Other religions, such as Buddhism, were brought from India by missionary monks. Over many centuries, these different traditions developed many similarities as their beliefs merged and mixed together.

Confucianism

At about the same time that the Buddha was preaching his message in India (*see pages 44–45*), two great religious teachers emerged in China: Confucius and Lao Tze, the founder of Taoism (*see pages 52–53*).

Confucius was born in 551 B.C.E. in north China. As a young man he became interested in finding the best way to behave and live in this world. He gave up his job in the government and dedicated himself to teaching people how to live in peace and harmony. Today, there are about 5 million Confucians in China and the Far East.

▶ **A traditional Confucian musician** in South Korea. In Confucianism, music and dance form an important part of the elaborate temple ceremonies.

▲ **These Confucian priests** are conducting a temple ceremony. After Confucius' death in 479 B.C.E., his followers built temples in his honour.

Confucian beliefs

Confucius believed that the way to live a better life was to respect other people and honour the memory of your ancestors. He taught five virtues which people should follow: kindness, righteousness, sobriety, wisdom and trustworthiness.

Confucians also believe in *Jen*, which is the principle of showing courtesy and loyalty to other people at all times. This is because Confucius taught that a person's own well-being depended directly on the well-being of others. His teachings influenced Chinese society so much that, right up to the beginning of this century, Chinese civil service exams were based on the thoughts of Confucius.

▼ **This Confucian temple,** with its winglike roof, is in Kunming, southwest China. Many temples were destroyed during China's Cultural Revolution of the 1960s. Some are now being restored to their former glory.

Rites, worship and scripture

Confucians consider the family and family values to be very important. Children are taught to respect their parents and elders, and to obey their wishes. Confucians worship their ancestors in temples or at altars in their homes.

Confucian scripture consists of five texts, which together are known as the Five Classics. These five collections of poems, historical records, rituals and sayings include many of the teachings of Confucius.

Taoism

The great Chinese religion of Taoism was founded in the sixth century B.C.E. by the philosopher Lao Tze, the Supreme Master, who lived at the same time as Confucius (*see pages 50–51*). Lao Tze taught about the *Tao*, or "Way", which is the underlying spiritual force of the universe that exists in all things. The goal of Taoists is to live in harmony with the *Tao*, in order to liberate the soul and become one of the Immortals. Today, Taoism is practised in Japan, Hong Kong, Taiwan, Malaysia and Vietnam, as well as in its native China.

Gods and Immortals

Lao Tze taught that there are no gods or goddesses, only the *Tao*. Later, however, Taoists began to worship Lao Tze himself and other important teachers, as well as the forces of nature, such as the sun, moon, stars and tides.

▶ **A statue of an Immortal** stands guard in the Man Mo temple, Hong Kong. Man is the god of literature and civil servants, while Mo is the god of martial arts.

▶ **According to legend,** Lao Tze left his job and rode off to the mountains in the west on the back of an ox. The guardian of the mountain pass asked him to write down his teachings, and this became the *Daodejing*, the sacred book of Taoism.

In their quest to become Immortals, some Taoists made great efforts to find an elixir (potion) that could give them eternal life.

Main beliefs

According to Taoist belief, the fate of the soul is determined by the good and evil actions a person does during his or her lifetime.

As a guide for living, Taoism forbids five things: telling lies, stealing, committing adultery, drinking alcohol and murder. There are also 10 guidelines to govern good deeds. These include obeying your elders, loving your parents, being tolerant, helping others and acting without thought for yourself.

Taoism also requires its followers to have good mental and physical control over themselves. People can develop this through a series of exercises called *T'ai chi*, or "shadow boxing". Millions of Chinese people still practice *T'ai chi* every day.

Festivals and rites

The most important Taoist festival is *Zhon-gyual*, which is celebrated on the 15th day of the 7th month. At this time, the hungry souls of the dead are said to appear in the world of the living, so that Taoist priests can free them from their suffering. The most important religious rite is *Jiao*. This is a ceremony to drive evil spirits out of the ground and leave it pure and clean.

▼ **Living in harmony** with the natural world is a central part of Taoist thought. Mountains, lakes, trees and waterfalls are considered particularly important.

▲ **The yin and yang symbol** represents the female (yin) and the male (yang) principles, which together are responsible for all creation. The many opposing but harmonious forces in nature are considered to be either yin or yang.

Shinto

Shinto, or the "way of the gods", is the ancient religion of Japan. Its followers believe in spirits, called *kami*, which live in animals, plants and natural places such as mountains, rivers and paddy fields. The spirits of great leaders and teachers can also become *kami*. The most important *kami* is Amaterasu, the sun goddess, who is believed to be the ancestor of the emperors of Japan. Another popular *kami* is Inari, the rice producer.

▲ **Mount Fuji,** Japan's most sacred mountain, has a Shinto shrine at its summit. Each year, millions of pilgrims make the steep climb to visit the shrine.

Creation myths

In Shinto myth, the Earth was created by the god Izanagi and his wife, Izanami. They stood on a rainbow called the Floating Bridge of Heaven and stirred the whirling waters below with a jewel-covered spear, bringing forth the islands that make up Japan.

The children of Izanagi and Izanami became the gods of nature. Izanami died while giving birth to the fire god, Kagutsuchi-no-kami. Izanagi tried in vain to bring his wife back from the Land of the Dead, and then plunged into the sea to wash away his grief and the corruption of the underworld. As he washed, the sun goddess, Amaterasu, was born from his left eye; the moon god, Tsukuyama, was born from his right eye; and the storm god, Susano, was born from his nose.

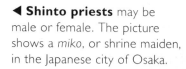

◀ **Shinto priests** may be male or female. The picture shows a *miko*, or shrine maiden, in the Japanese city of Osaka.

◄ **These children** are taking part in the Grand Festival at the Toshugu shrine, Nikko, in May. The shrine is dedicated to the kami of a 17th-century military leader.

The most important shrine in Japan is at Ise and it is dedicated to Amaterasu. Tradition says that the inner shrine at Ise must be destroyed every 20 years and then rebuilt nearby in exactly the same style, but using new wood and materials.

Shinto festivals

Each shrine has an annual festival, during which people flock to the shrine to pay their respects to the *kami* and to eat, drink and enjoy themselves. A portable shrine is carried through the streets to make sure that the *kami's* blessing is bestowed on the whole community, so that no one misses out.

Visiting a shrine

All over Japan, there are many thousands of shrines (about 80,000 altogether) dedicated to the various *kami*. Visiting the shrines is a central part of Shinto worship. People enter the shrine along a straight path. They wash at a water trough to purify themselves and then hang up wooden tablets with prayers written on them. Next, they proceed to the inner shrine, where a sacred symbol of the *kami,* such as a mirror or sword, is kept. They summon the *kami* with a bell and offer it gifts of money or rice. Then they bow twice, clap twice to welcome the *kami* and bow once again. The *kami* can also be worshipped at home, and many people have small wooden shrines in their houses.

▶ **The entrance** to a Shinto shrine is marked by a wooden gateway, or *torii*, which separates the sacred world of the shrine from the world outside.

Zen Buddhism

▲ **This statue shows** Amida Buddha, the central figure of the Pure Land School, one of the most important Buddhist groups in Japan.

Buddhism began in India in the sixth century B.C.E. (*see pages 44–47*). Buddhist monks brought it to Japan in about 550 C.E. from China and Korea. Today, there are millions of Japanese Buddhists. Many different Buddhist groups flourish in Japan. All of them belong to the Mahayana school of Buddhism (*see page 46*), but they have different ways of practising. One of the biggest and best-known of these groups is Zen, which means "meditation".

The Zen masters

The two great Zen teachers were Eisai (1141–1215) and Dogen (1200–1253). Both Eisai and Dogen introduced new ideas about the practice of meditation, which is at the heart of Zen Buddhism.

Meditation is a way of concentrating and focusing the mind to achieve an inner stillness that leads to the state of enlightenment (spiritual awakening). Eisai's new way of helping people to concentrate was to pose them riddles that challenged the way they thought about things. For example: "What is the sound of one hand clapping?"

◀ **These Zen monks** in Kyoto, Japan, are wearing traditional monks' clothes.

FLOWER FESTIVAL

Every spring, on 8 April, Japanese Buddhists celebrate a flower festival called Hana Matsuri. The festival is held to mark the Buddha's birthday. Temples are decorated with cherry blossoms, and children pour scented tea over an image of the baby Buddha. Food stalls, dancers and acrobats make sure it is a happy day for everyone. These children are wearing paper flowers in their hair to celebrate this special day.

▼ **A Buddhist pagoda,** or shrine. This one forms part of the Yakushiji temple in Japan and is unusual because it has three pairs of roofs. Most pagodas have five roofs. The spire symbolises wisdom, while the five tiered roofs represent the five basic elements of the universe – earth, water, fire, wind and emptiness.

▼ **Most Zen monasteries** include a sand garden, whose rocks and raked sand represent the simple lines and proportions of a natural landscape or the ocean.

Monks and nuns

Zen monks and nuns live in monasteries where they lead simple lives, based around meditation and work. Their few possessions include a conical straw hat to shield them from the sun, a black robe, a pair of wicker sandals and a cloth bag for receiving alms (gifts of food and money). Both monks and nuns shave their heads to show that they have given up their worldly lives.

Meditation

Zen Buddhists believe meditation brings a better understanding of life and greater self-awareness. There are many techniques that help people to meditate by making them focus their minds. They include sitting beside or tending a sand garden, which is an arrangement of rocks and sand that represents natural features such as mountains and ocean waves.

Martial arts such as karate and sports such as archery are also popular, because they teach mental and physical control, and so require strong concentration.

Other aids to meditation include short verses called *haikus*. These point the way to understanding in as few words as possible. This haiku was written in the 17th century:

> *"The still pond, ah!*
> *A frog jumps in.*
> *The water's sound."*

SPIRIT RELIGIONS

IN PLACES WHERE PEOPLE LIVE CLOSE TO NATURE AND RELY ON NATURE ALONE for their food and survival, the natural world is both feared and revered. In these parts of the world, people's traditional beliefs are often based upon the worship of spirits that live in animals, trees and the landscape.

▲ **Smoking a sacred pipe,** such as the one above, is believed to bring the members of North American tribes together and unite them with the spirits and the universe.

South America

For the people of the South American rainforest, the forest animals and trees are powerful spirits that must be respected. The most powerful animal spirit is that of the jaguar – the largest and most feared jungle hunter. The *shaman*, or witch doctor, of the tribe is believed to be able to turn into a jaguar in order to visit the spirit world. To achieve this transformation, he dresses in jaguar skins and a necklace of jaguar teeth. He may even growl like a jaguar. Then, in a deep trance, he asks the spirits to grant favours for his tribe, such as sending more animals to hunt or curing sickness and disease.

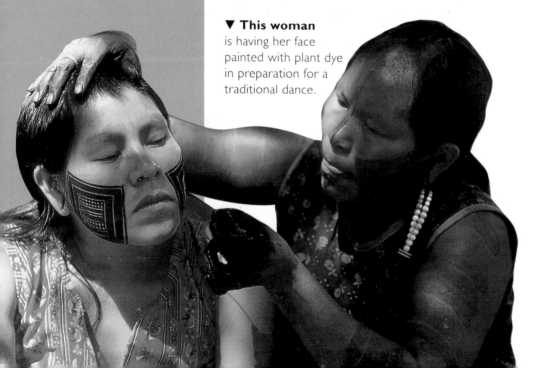

▼ **This woman** is having her face painted with plant dye in preparation for a traditional dance.

Dance and ceremony

The rainforest people believe that music summons the spirits. Because of this, special events – such as initiation rites (when boys have to prove their courage), births and honey gathering – are always celebrated with music and dancing.

When a person dies, singing and dancing are thought to speed the soul to heaven. The dancers wear elaborate make-up and costumes that they believe give them magical powers. They are accompanied by musicians playing bamboo flutes, reed pipes, horns and shell whistles.

North America

There are many different groups practising spirit religions in North America, and each has its own distinctive beliefs and ceremonies. Most, however, share the belief in a supreme being, called the Great Spirit, who created the Earth. They also believe that every living thing has a spirit, which may be good or evil. Their beliefs are reflected in their many myths and legends.

◀ **The animals carved** on totem poles represent guardian spirits of a tribe. This totem pole carving shows an eagle.

Native North Americans

While the Great Spirit rules over the world, Native Americans (once called Indians) believe that the day-to-day running of the Earth is left to the spirits of nature.

One such spirit is the spirit of thunder, which takes the form of a mighty eagle called the Thunderbird. The beating of its wings sounds like thunderclaps, while lightning flashes from its eyes and beak. Although it is awesome, the Thunderbird is also a welcome spirit, because it brings rain to water the crops. It also fights the evil spirits of the underworld. Anyone struck by the Thunderbird's lightning is believed to possess special spiritual powers.

Inuit beliefs

Traditionally, the Inuit peoples of the Arctic (some of whom are known as Eskimos) survived in their harsh environment by hunting the animals around them, such as whales, walruses, seals and polar bears.

According to Inuit belief, every animal has a spirit. This makes the relationship between the hunter and the hunted a very special one. When an animal is killed, the hunters dance and sing to thank its spirit for giving them meat and skins, and to express the hope that the spirit will return to be hunted again.

▼ **By beating a special drum,** an Inuit *shaman* (witch doctor) enters a trance and can travel to the spirit world.

▲ **This young man of the Pawnee tribe** is wearing ceremonial dress. Traditionally, when boys reached manhood, they went to the forest to seek out their own guardian spirit, which sometimes appeared in the form of an animal.

Africa

Africa is a vast continent with a huge variety of beliefs. Many Africans are Muslims or Christians, but there are many others who still follow traditional African spirit religions. They believe in a Great God who created the world, and in many lesser gods of thunder, rain, rivers and so on. In addition to these, there are thousands of spirits of nature. People also believe that the spirits of their dead ancestors continue to live among them.

▲ **This miniature mask,** called a "passport" mask, is used to show that the owner possesses a full-sized mask. Passport masks are also used as magic charms.

▶ **This clay figure represents Ale,** the Earth goddess of Nigeria's Ibo people. She is believed to make the crops grow and protect the harvest. She is sometimes shown with a child on her knees, because she is also the goddess who brings children into the world.

Witch doctors

In traditional African society, the witch doctor was one of the most important members of the community and was greatly respected for his wisdom. He used his great knowledge of nature to cure the sick by concocting medicines from plants, roots and berries. He also cured those who were thought to have been bewitched by evil spirits or the souls of their enemies.

Witch doctors are still very important in many parts of Africa. They are often asked for their advice and guidance, perhaps to intervene in a quarrel or put a curse on an enemy! In desert regions, they interpret the will of the gods from the tracks left by animals in the sand. Witch doctors may even be asked to appear at important state occasions to give the events their blessing and to ward off evil spirits.

◀ **A witch doctor's store** of plants and potions in Zambia.

Masks and fetishes

Wooden spirit masks are often worn by dancers during religious rituals and ceremonies. Animal masks are thought to make the wearer strong and protect them from evil, because the power of an animal's spirit is concentrated in its head. The dancers may also wear masks that represent their ancestors.

A fetish is any object that is believed to have magical powers. Some fetishes are linked with a particular spirit, whose wishes they are believed to carry out.

Australasia

The peoples of Australia, New Zealand and the islands of the South Pacific have a rich mythology. There are many shared themes, because explorers and traders exchanged stories as they went from island to island. But each region also has its own special spirits and religious tales that seek to explain the origins of the world and the people in it. Passed on by word of mouth, many have been told, almost unchanged, for thousands of years.

▲ **These dancers** from Papua New Guinea are wearing traditional ceremonial dress.

Dreamtime
The Aborigines of Australia believe that the world was made long ago, during the Dreamtime. This was when spirits called the Ancestors travelled across Australia, shaping the landscape. Aborigines believe that the land is sacred and must be cared for, because it is part of them, and they are part of it. Special occasions are marked by acting out episodes from the Dreamtime.

Maori creation myths
In many myths, including those told by the Maoris of New Zealand, the islands of the South Pacific were fished from the depths of the sea by the ocean spirit Maui, who mistook them for a giant fish. Another story tells how Maui created day and night by tricking his grandfather, the spirit of the sun, into travelling more slowly across the sky.

▼ **Uluru (Ayers Rock)** is the most sacred Aborigine site.

Spirits of the sea
The sea plays a vital part in the lives of the South Pacific islanders. They rely on it for food and respect its awesome power. Many of the gods they worship are spirits of the sea. Among the most important are the shark gods who guard each of the islands. The Fijian god of fishing, Dekuwaqa, takes the form of a gigantic basking shark.

◄ **This carved statue** of the ocean spirit Maui is in a Maori meeting house in New Zealand.

NEW RELIGIONS

THROUGHOUT HISTORY, NEW RELIGIOUS GROUPS HAVE CONTINUED TO emerge. Some have developed within established religions, remaining part of the "parent" religion and sharing many of its practices. Others have broken away completely, to become independent religions in their own right, with their own set of beliefs and practices. There is also a number of entirely new religions, with new leaders and rituals, and fresh ways of looking at the crucial issues of life.

▲ **Ras ("Prince") Tafari** became Emperor Haile Selassie I of Ethiopia in 1930. He died in 1975.

Rastafarianism

The Rastafarian faith began in Jamaica, in the West Indies. The religion's beliefs are based on the Bible, which is widely read and debated, mixed with many African beliefs and traditions.

Rastafarians (or Rastas for short) worship Emperor Haile Selassie of Ethiopia as their Messiah and leader. They see themselves as one of the 12 tribes of ancient Israel, and consider Ethiopia to be their "promised land" (*see page 18*). One day, they believe, they will return to Ethiopia from exile in the countries to which their ancestors were taken as slaves. Rastas call such places of exile "Babylon".

There are no Rastafarian churches. People meet up to pray to *Jah*, or God, and to sing and play music. Reggae music, which has become famous all over the world, is seen as a mark of Rastafarian culture and identity. Today, many Rastafarians live in the U.S.A., Canada and Britain, as well as in the West Indies.

◀ **Many Rastafarians grow their hair** into long twists called dreadlocks and do not cut their beards, in accordance with a verse in the Bible. Dreadlocks are supposed to inspire respect, or "dread", in other people.

Baha'ism

The Baha'i faith developed in Persia (modern-day Iran) in the 19th century. Its first preachers were a holy man called the Bab and one of his most devoted followers, Baha'u'llah. The Bab saw himself as the latest in a long line of spiritual leaders, while Baha'u'llah declared himself to be a prophet, sent to lead the world into a new age.

Both men taught that all religions are divine, and that all the great prophets – such as Muhammad, Jesus and Buddha –

Hare Krishna

The proper name of the movement popularly known as Hare Krishna is the International Society for Krishna Consciousness (ISKCON). The movement was founded in 1966 by a Hindu holy man named Bhaktivedanta Swami Prabhupada.

The Swami left India to come to the West, where he attracted thousands of followers, including members of the Beatles rock group. He taught that people should give up their attachment to the material world and concentrate instead on achieving greater self-awareness and inner peace. To help them in this task, they must give up meat, alcohol, drugs and gambling.

Many male Hare Krishna followers shave their heads as a sign of cleanliness and to show that they have given up worldly concerns.

They chant the names of the Hindu gods Krishna and Rama as a sign of their devotion.

were servants of the same God and preached the same message. They believed that each religion is like a chapter in a book, with many more chapters still to be written. Their mission was to bring peace to the world and to unite all religions and races.

Today, there are approximately 3.5 million Baha'is throughout the world. Despite suffering persecution in Iran, Baha'is still see themselves as World Citizens and continue to spread their twin messages of peace and unity. The largest Baha'i group is in India, where the religion has about one million followers.

Baha'is gather in homes and at temples, called Houses of Worship, to pray together at informal services. There are no priests because all Baha'is consider themselves as equal before God.

▲ **Like all Baha'i temples,** the Baha'i lotus temple in Delhi, India, has a nine-sided design. Similar lotus temples have been built in Europe and Australia.

▼ **Hare Krishna followers** dance, chant their *mantra* (sacred song) and play cymbals and drums as they parade through the streets.

Mennonites and Amish

Many new religious movements have developed from mainstream Christianity. The Mennonite Church grew out of a group of radical Christian reformers during the first half of the 16th century.

Mennonites accept Jesus Christ as their saviour and guide, and obey the word of the Bible. They also believe in baptising adults, rather than children, and in keeping separate from the outside world, because salvation can only be gained within their own community.

There are Mennonites in many countries, but they are most numerous in North America. There are currently about 1,250,000 Mennonites throughout the world.

A stricter group of Mennonites, called the Amish Order, emerged in the 1690s. Most Amish now live in the U.S.A., in small settlements of up to 200 people. They have no churches, but gather in each other's homes to worship.

Like the Mennonites, the Amish separate themselves from the rest of society. They wear traditional clothes: Amish men wear broad-brimmed black hats, while women wear long dresses, bonnets and shawls. The Amish also refuse to use "modern" machinery and technology such as electric tools, televisions and telephones.

▲ **Members of the Amish Order** have a reputation as hard workers. This Amish carpenter is making a wheel in his workshop in Pennsylvania, U.S.A.

Mormons

The Mormon movement, or the Church of Jesus Christ of Latter Day Saints, was founded in New York in 1830 by a man named Joseph Smith. Smith claimed that when he was 18, an angel had appeared to him and revealed to him the Book of Mormon, an ancient Biblical text. Mormons base their faith and their way of life on this book.

Joseph Smith's first followers were badly persecuted, so they fled west across the United States to seek a better life. They finally reached the state of Utah, where they built Salt Lake City – their new headquarters.

Mormons believe in hard work and value a good education. They do not smoke and are not allowed to drink alcohol, tea or coffee.

◄ **The Mormon temple** in Manti, Utah, U.S.A., is used for religious ceremonies. The site was dedicated to the Mormon Church by Brigham Young (1801–1877), a religious leader.

New Age

A wide variety of beliefs and groups make up the New Age Movement, which draws on ideas and insights from many different religious traditions.

The Findhorn Community is a New Age group founded in Scotland in 1965 by Eileen and Peter Caddy. Its followers believe that the natural world is under the control of spirits who send messages to this world through the Findhorn members.

▲ **Members of the Findhorn Community** worship together through dancing, prayer and meditation.

Other New Age groups use healing, astrology and crystals to get in touch with the spirit world and the creative forces of the universe. Many New Age followers practise meditation so that they can reach their inner souls and transform their lives for the better.

Unification Church

In 1954, the Reverend Sun Myung Moon founded a new religious group in Korea, called the Unification Church (now widely known as the "Moonies"). Its main teaching is The Divine Principle, which was revealed to the Reverend Moon in a series of visions. His followers believe that the Reverend Moon is the Lord of the Second Advent, who will create the perfect family and so save the human race. Large rallies, lecture tours and mass weddings are all part of spreading the message. Some people have criticised the Unification Church, alleging that people are "brainwashed" into joining the movement, although the Unification Church strongly denies this.

◀ **Thousands of "Moonie" couples** take part in a mass wedding in the rain. The couples are chosen for each other by the Reverend Moon himself. Every bride and groom wears identical clothes, so that no couple stands out as more important than the rest.

Glossary

Many words describing the customs and ideas of individual religions are explained in the text. Try looking in the index if you cannot find the word you are looking for here.

afterlife Life after death. Many religions believe that a person's soul lives on after his or her physical body has died.

altar A table in a place of worship, at which offerings are made to God or to a deity.

ancestor A person who lived a long time ago and from whom you are descended. In some religions, people worship their ancestors.

astrology The study of the stars, planets and heavenly bodies, and the effect they have on people's lives and personalities.

blasphemy Treating a sacred being or object in an impolite or disrespectful manner.

blessing The approval or good favour of God or of a deity.

charm An object, such as a mask, statue or trinket, that is believed to have special powers. Charms are used to ward off evil.

chastity Being pure and virtuous. Monks and nuns often take a vow of chastity, which means that they cannot get married.

covenant An agreement. In Judaism, God entered into a covenant with the Jews, promising to protect and bless them as long as they worshipped no other gods.

cremation The burning of a body after death.

deity Another name for a god, goddess or sacred being.

devotion Worshipping a deity with great love and loyalty.

disciple A follower of a religious leader or a particular religious teaching.

enlightenment Realising the truth behind everything in the world, after many years of prayer and meditation, as if you have woken up from a deep sleep.

eternal Something that lasts forever.

faith Having a firm belief in, and commitment to, a deity or a particular religious teaching.

fasting Going without food. Fasting is an important part of many religious festivals and ceremonies.

fertility Productiveness or fruitfulness. In ancient times, people prayed to fertility gods and goddesses to make their crops grow.

festival A day or several days of celebration. Festivals are often held to celebrate events in a deity's life, such as the deity's birth or death, and to mark important times of the year, such as New Year and the coming of spring.

God A supreme being who created the world and who controls everything in it. God is believed to be all-seeing, all-knowing and all-powerful.

gods Sacred beings with divine powers, who are often seen as different aspects of a supreme being. Female gods are called goddesses.

heaven The home of God or of the gods, which is usually believed to be in the sky. In many religions, heaven is thought to be a happy, blissful place to which the souls of good and godly people go when they die.

horoscope A chart showing the position of the stars and planets at the time of a person's birth. It is used in some religions to fix auspicious (lucky) dates for weddings and other important events.

idol A statue of a deity.

immortal Living forever. In many religions, the gods are believed to be immortal.

incarnation An appearance of a god on Earth in human form. For example, Hindus believe that the god Vishnu has appeared in several incarnations to save the Earth from disaster, while Christians believe that Jesus Christ was the incarnation of God.

initiation rite A ceremony that marks the start of a child's adult life or membership of a faith community.

meditation Thinking and concentrating very deeply to clear and focus the mind.

Messiah A Hebrew word which means the person chosen by God to be king. The Jews believe that the Messiah is yet to come, while the Christian Bible says that Jesus Christ was the Messiah.

missionary A person who travels from place to place teaching people about their religion.

monk A man who gives up his possessions and ties with the world and devotes his life to God or to a deity. He lives as part of a religious order and takes vows which usually include poverty, chastity and obedience.

monotheistic religion A religion based on the belief in one supreme God. Islam, Judaism and Christianity are all monotheistic religions.

mummy A dead body covered with oil and wrapped in bandages to stop it from rotting. In ancient Egypt, it was thought that unless a body was mummified, the dead person's soul would not survive to enter the next world.

myth A sacred story that explains natural phenomena, such as the weather, night and day, and the seasons, as the work of the gods.

mythology The study of myths, often incorporating folk stories and religious beliefs.

nun A woman who gives up her possessions and ties with the world and devotes her life to God or to a deity (*see* monk).

offering A gift – such as fruit, flowers, incense or money – that is offered to the gods as thanks, or in return for their blessing.

parable A story told to teach a religious lesson. Parables were often based on events in everyday life, so that their message would be easier to understand.

persecute To treat someone badly because of their religious (or political) beliefs.

pilgrimage A special journey to a sacred place such as a shrine, a holy mountain or the tomb of a saint. A person who goes on a pilgrimage is called a pilgrim.

prayer Talking to God or to a deity. In prayer, people worship, ask for help and advice, and give thanks for what they have received. Worshippers can pray in public or private using set prayers or their own words and thoughts.

preaching Religious teaching.

priest A man who conducts religious services and acts as a spiritual guide for worshippers. A female priest is a priestess.

prophet A person who speaks for God or for a deity. For example, Muhammad is the Prophet of Islam to whom Allah revealed his wishes for the world.

pulpit A raised platform in a place of worship from which the preacher delivers a sermon.

rebirth The rebirth of a person's soul into another body when the person dies.

reincarnation (*see* rebirth).

righteousness Goodness or holiness.

rite A religious ceremony.

ritual (*see* rite).

sacred Another word for holy.

sacrifice An animal or person offered to a god to gain favour.

salvation Being saved from sin, or breaking free of the cycle of birth and rebirth and gaining enlightenment.

saviour Someone who brings salvation. Christians, for example, believe that Jesus Christ is their saviour, because he saved the world from sin.

scripture Sacred writings.

sermon A religious talk given in a place of worship.

shrine A place of worship, which may be part of a church or temple or in the home.

sin A wrong or wicked action.

soul The innermost part of a person or animal, which is distinct from the physical body.

spirit Another name for the soul (*see above*). In some religions, the spirits of animals and natural places, such as rivers and mountains, are worshipped as gods.

temple A place of worship that is believed to be the earthly home of a god or goddess.

tomb A grave or burial place.

totem A plant or animal that is the emblem of a tribe or clan and their guardian spirit.

underworld For the ancient Egyptians, a place where people went to when they died.

wisdom Great knowledge and understanding of a subject.

worship Showing love and devotion to God or to a deity through prayer, offerings, hymns and daily living.

Index

Note: Page numbers in *italic* refer to information given only in boxes or in picture captions or labels.

PICTURE ACKNOWLEDGEMENTS

Marion Appleton, 10 (bottom), 13, 16 (centre), 18, 35, 49, 50 (bottom left), 60 (top right), 64 (bottom left), 67 (top right); *Roy Flooks,* black line icons *Andre Hrydziusko,* 11 (bottom); *John James,* (Temple Rogers Artists' Agents) 12, 18–19, 24–25, 30–31, 36, 46, 51, 57; *Peter Sarson,* 10 (top left); *Nadine Wickenden,* 14–15, 14 (top left), 21 (top right), 27 (bottom centre), 28 (top left), 29 (top right), 34 (centre right), 39 (bottom left), 42 (left), 44 (bottom), 54 (left).

PHOTOGRAPHS

t = top, b = bottom, c = centre, l = left, r = right

2–3 Mark Cator/Impact; 8 t Mark Henley/Impact, b Mark Cator/Impact; 9 Steve Parry/Impact; 10 Nigel Francis/Robert Harding Picture Library; 12 Ancient Art & Architecture Collection; 13 (both) Werner Forman Archive; 14 l Robert Harding Picture Library, r Michael Holford; 15 l Richard Ashworth/Robert Harding Picture Library, r Adam Woolfitt/Robert Harding Picture Library; 16 Index/Bridgeman Art Library; 17 t British Library/Bridgeman Art Library, b Mark Henley/Impact; 18 Robert Harding Picture Library; 20 t Yoram Lehmann/Robert Harding Picture Library, b Robert Francis/Robert Harding Picture Library; 21 t Photri/Robert Harding Picture Library, b Zefa; 22 t Victoria & Albert Museum/Bridgeman Art Library, b Barry Searle/Sonia Halliday Photographs; 23 t AKG London, b Giraudon/Bridgeman Art Library; 24 t Homer Sykes/Impact, b Penny Tweedie/Impact; 26 t Fred Friberg/Robert Harding Picture Library, b Mohamed Ansar/Impact; 27 Robert Frerck/Robert Harding Picture Library; 28 Christophe Bluntzer/Impact; 29 t Library of Escorial/Michael Holford, b Javed A. Jafferji/Impact; 30 Peter Keen/Comstock; 31 James Strachan/Robert Harding Picture Library; 32 l Mohamed Ansar/Impact, r Mohamed Abu Mustafa; 32–33 Mohamed Ansar/Impact; 33 Abbas/Magnum; 34 l Robert Harding Picture Library, r Bryan Parsley/Tony Stone Images; 35 Sassoon/Robert Harding Picture Library; 36 Sunil Gupta/Network; 37 t Robert Harding Picture Library, b British Library/Michael Holford; 38 t Andrea Booher/Tony Stone Images, b Duncan Maxwell/Robert Harding Picture Library; 39 t Corbis/Bettmann/UPI, b Grilly Bernard/Tony Stone Images; 40 J.H.C. Wilson/Robert Harding Picture Library; 40–41 Robert Harding Picture Library; 41 Jehangir Gazdar/Comstock; 42 Ann & Bury Peerless; 43 t Ann & Bury Peerless, b Robert Harding Picture Library; 44 Hugh Sitton/Tony Stone Images; 45 t Anders H. Andersen/Tibet Image Bank, b James Strachan/Tony Stone Images; 46 Alain Le Garsmeur/Tony Stone Images; 47 t Robert Harding Picture Library, b Soifer/Bushnell/Tony Stone Images; 48 t Dilip Mehta/Colorific!, b Ann & Bury Peerless; 49 Tony Stone Images; 50 Michael Macintyre/Hutchison Library; 51 Hutchison Library; 52 l Oriental Museum/University of Durham, r Richard Greenhill; 52–53 Keren Su/Tony Stone Images; 54 Robert Francis/Hutchison Library; 55 l Graham Harrison, r Tony Stone Images; 56 t Jean Paul Navicet/Colorific!; 56 b Patricio Goycoolea/Hutchison Library; 57 t Jon Burbank/Hutchison Library, b Graham Harrison; 58 t Museum of the American Indian, Heye Foundation, New York/Werner Forman Archive, b Tom Kelly/Impact; 59 t Hutchison Library, b l R.W. Jones/Robert Harding Picture Library, b r Bryan & Cherry Alexander; 60 t Werner Forman Archive, b David Reed/Impact; 61 t Carolyn Bates/Impact, c Robert Harding Picture Library, b Michael Botham/Robert Harding Picture Library; 62 t AKG London, b Alain Le Garsmeur/Impact; 63 t Christopher Rennie/Robert Harding Picture Library, b Ian Summer/Robert Harding Picture Library; 64 Sylvain Grandadam/Colorific!; 65 t Homer Sykes/Impact, b Gideon Mendel/Network.